Social skills games for elementary and middle school kids

91 games to improve all-around skills in elementary school children and teens

Dorothy J. Winfrey

Contents

Social skills games for elementary school children

ames are a part of childhood and are fundamental for their integral development. They are a perfect tool when it comes to developing social skills that will help the child build positive relationships and learn to get along with others.

Currently, pedagogy makes use of all kinds of recreational activities that motivate and enable students to learn more effectively. Teaching them while having fun will positively enhance their learning process.

Teaching them while they delight will mark their process positively, thus helping them to learn quickly.

The game, today represents an educational objective, it by itself, has the ability to teach, without the need for accessories, a child who is open to the game, will be able to learn in total freedom.

When it comes to learning, it is not only about acquiring a simple knowledge or achieving certain skills, the game also helps them in their psychomotor, cognitive and physical development, favoring affective bonds with their parents and their environment as well as socializing with others.

Children invest a lot of time in games, in fact, there are countless numbers of games adapted to different needs, ages and skills; more than fun, they are motivational and encouraging.

Jean Piaget (1956), psychologist, affirms that games are part of a child's intelligence, since it represents a functional or reproductive assimilation of reality, according to each individual's evolutionary stage.

For Lev Semyonovich Vigotsky (1924), also a psychologist, games arise from a child's need to interact with others, where play is a critical role in the child's learning process.

Zapata Rafael (1990), writer, expresses that play is a fundamental element in education; children learn more while playing, which is why this activity should become the central axis of the program.

Jerome Bruner (1974), psychologist, considered games as a format of communicative activity, intended to continuously and spontaneously restructure children's different points of view and knowledge, while having fun and enjoying the wonderful experience of being together and forging spaces of interesting growth.

By incorporating these games into the school system and not just at home, children can begin to imitate reality, representing what they want to live or experience, and allowing them the opportunity to freely express their emotions.

Parents have the responsibility of encouraging children to want to participate in games, in their different environments, so that they become familiar with them and give rise to a unique teaching-learning process.

.

Advantages of play in children's education

Games and play time in early childhood education:

- Increase well-being and freedom of expression. This is one of the most important stages of their life, there is no room for adult problems; innocence and play is everything.

- Promote social skills when interacting with other children, making it easier to share and exchange ideas and opinions, and establish relationships.

- Allow better decision making and responsibility, learning to think before acting and assuming the consequences of their actions when the game ends.

- Help children mature thanks to the fact that during play, children must learn to think, analyze, and wait, all actions that as they grow up they will need to apply in their daily lives.

- Allow children to begin to explore the world that surrounds them. Due to the different spaces in which games take place, the child will be able to discover the characteristics of each one through exploration.

- Help develop creativity and imagination. These types of skills should be stimulated at a young age, so that they do not become a problem and limitation in adult life.
- Improve understanding; learning that things can happen in different ways helps children process information and understand future events or occurrences.

How does play contribute in children's abilities?

When play is used as an indispensable tool in childhood, children develop and strengthen their capacities:

- Physical, since, due to the different movements, they exercise and contribute to their psychomotor coordination, reducing the risk of becoming obese children and giving them a restful night's sleep, since sleep is stimulated.
- Sensory and mental, when coming into contact with different shapes, textures, sizes, smells and colors, it is favored.
- Affective, they learn to experience and express their emotions independently.

There are many capacities that each child has, and through the different games their integral formation is consolidated to make them child models in each context in which they develop.

Each and every one of these playful activities has become a main tool in the development of children's intelligence.

For this reason, parents, teachers, guides or counselors are then provided with different tools that allow them to make their training process an extraordinary adventure.

Relationship building games

The best way to build relationships is through play, since children can function freely. This allows for a healthy development and increases the ability to bond with others

1.- Reflection of the week

Requirements: sheet of paper, pencil

Number of players: 10 - 15 children

The group leader will place all the children in a circle and explain the game instructions.

Then, will proceed to give each child a sheet of paper and pencil, explaining that they must write three events that they have experienced during the week. Two of them will be bad experiences and the other will be good. When describing the two bad events, they must express why they think they were bad and what they learned from it.

Once they have finished writing, they will proceed to share their experiences aloud with the rest of the group.

This will allow the children to understand that everyone goes through difficult times, but despite them, there is always something good. Even if it's small and insignificant, it is a reason to smile and be grateful.

When everyone is silent, the guide will open a space for questions and answers in order to deepen the learning process.

How did you feel talking about your experience? Do you think your experiences are unique? Are they easier or tougher than the others? What did you think when you heard your classmates' situations? What would you do instead?

This exercise will not only help the child reflect, but also get to know others and interact.

2.- The bag

Requirements: objects and bags

Number of players: 5 - 10 children

Each child, prior to the game, should bring from home objects that are of great value to them and place them in a bag. These objects must have specific characteristics that allow the child to define the importance they have in their life.

Once the game begins, the guide will divide the class into groups of 5. Then the students will proceed to take the items from their bags to share with their group. This will allow them to initiate conversation and get to know one another.

Each child will have the opportunity to participate. The game can vary and the children can rotate groups in order to interact with other classmates.

After the activity, the leader will open a space for questions and answers.

What did you think of the activity? How did you feel about sharing your experiences? Did you enjoy showing and talking about your valuables? Why?

It is a space for interaction, in which the child can deeply relate with their environment.

3.– I am

Requirements: sheets of bond paper, markers, tape.

Number of players: 5 – 10 children

Each child must bring a sheet of bond paper and markers. This activity will enhance their personal growth.

The leader or guide will explain that on this sheet, they will write a short description of themselves, what they feel and what they like.

For instance:

I love when...

_____

Sometimes I wonder if...

_____

I would like to..._____

I am happy when...

_____

I like...

_____

It saddens me_

_____

When I grow up I want_

_____

It scares me_

_____

The child will write everything they can think of that describes them. When finished, they will take their bond paper and with plastic tape place it, visibly, on the wall.

The leader will then call on each child to present to the rest of the class what they have written. During this time, the other children can ask for permission to speak and add characteristics that they believe also define the student that is presenting.

When everyone has participated, the guide will proceed to ask them: How did you feel? Do you think the characteristics expressed really define you? What do you think of what your classmates have added? What do you think of your classmate's personality?

These are just some questions that can guide the closing of the game, leading the children to achieve the proposed objective of getting to know one another through conversation.

.

4.– Who is who?

Requirements: Paper sheets and pencils

Number of players: 5 – 10 children

The group leader will give the children sheets of paper and a pencil; they will write a series of random characteristics and a blank line next to each, where they will place one of their classmates name.

Example:

He has two brothers: Mary

Loves the beach: Peter

Always arrives early: Robert

And so it will be done successively with each characteristic and each child. Everyone will be able to participate and identify the classmate they think the description is referring to.

This activity ends with the acquired learning, through questions and answers. How did you feel during the activity? Do you think your peers know you? Have you found an error in your description? Do you think your classmates know you well enough? Do you think it's necessary to share a little more?

This way, the importance of establishing relationships with others in the different spaces in which they operate is emphasized.

Games to
develop communication skills

Any effective communication process must take place early on in childhood, thus guaranteeing the child's optimal development in their environment.

Knowing how it should be carried out, as well as making use of each of its elements, is essential; a child who knows how to communicate is a happy child..

5.- Mimics

Requirements: objects that the child wants, notebook, pencil, sheets of paper, colors

Number of players: 5 – 15 children

The group leader will write different actions on several sheets of paper, and then proceed to form small groups. Each group will get a role with an action, and in a few minutes, they will have to create and represent the assigned action through mimics.

The rest of the observing group will be tasked with deciphering what is being communicated.

Each group will take their place in front of the class and act out their part, trying to transmit the message.

To conclude, the leader will ask the following questions: What did you think of the activity? How did you feel? Were the messages difficult to decipher? Why is it important to communicate? Do you think everyone has understood you?

Communicating is an essential action in the human being; effective communication must be promoted from childhood.

6.- What would you do if?

Requirements: sheets of paper and pencils

Number of players: 5 - 10 children.

The leader will be in charge of placing the children in groups, and little by little, will read some actions in which the children will have to place the answers on their sheets.

Example: What would you do if Mary fell in the yard?

What would you do if Charles couldn't go to the park with you?

What would you do if Daniela invited you to eat?

This is how the game works; each child must give an answer that they consider is the most appropriate.

Finally, once everyone has spoken, the leader will begin asking them different questions.

How did you feel communicating your thoughts? Do you think they are important? Why is it good to express what you think? What if we don't communicate our ideas?

The activity concludes by teaching the children the importance of communication.

.

7.- Resolve the conflict

Requirements: sheets of paper, pencils and colors

Number of players: 5 - 10 children

Requirements: sheets of paper, pencils and colors.

Number of players: 5 - 10 children.

The group leader will be in charge of dividing the children into small groups; each group will be told a different conflict and will be indicated to think of a timely solution for it.

A reasonable time will be set for them to think and generate the answer; after the time is up, each group will participate by explaining why they think their solution is the correct one.

When everyone has participated, questions will be asked in order to generate more communication between them.

Do you think your solution is the most effective? Why? If you had to provide another solution, what would it be? How do you feel about actively participating in conflict resolution?

In this way, the game will end by explaining to the children the importance of communicating freely with the other.

8.– The debate

Requirements: paper and pencil

Number of players: 5 - 10 children

The group guide will distribute the children into two teams and will indicate a topic of their interest to discuss.

They will be allocated a reasonable time to converse, using all the information they have about that topic.

After times up, a space will be open for discussion, in which, through questions and answers, they can debate and share their different opinions.

At the end, they will be asked about how they felt. What do you think of your classmate's answer in relation to a topic that is of interest to you? What can you add to your classmate's opinion? Do you think it is important to communicate your points of view?

The activity ends, emphasizing the importance and significance of communication on a day-to-day basis.

.

Managing emotions games

Emotions are normal and good to the extent of knowing how to channel them; therefore, the best moment to learn how to do this is at a young age.

In that manner, by children recognizing what they are feeling, they will be able to handle these emotions appropriately and prevent internal conflicts that tend to appear when they are mishandled.

9.– The dictionary

Requirements: paper sheet and pencil

Number of players: 10 – 15 children

The group guide will talk to the children about emotions and the importance of identifying them on a regular basis. Then will proceed to tell the class that they must make a small dictionary where they will write each of the emotions they know of and give a small definition; Love, joy, sadness, fear and more.

Once finished, the children will share their definitions with the class and establish differences and similarities between what they have written.

What are your emotions? How did you identify and define them? Why did you give that definition? What makes you feel like this? Are your emotions similar to your classmates?

By sharing, they will be able to identify these emotions and, in turn, express them when they arise. This will allow them to educate themselves on the subject and mange each one appropriately.

10.– The tale of emotions

Requirements: a story, paper and pencil

Number of participants: 5 – 10 children

The guide will sit the children in a large circle and read them a story, indicating that they must listen, identify and write down the emotions present in it.

Then, everyone will participate by not only mentioning the emotions in the story, but explaining why they think that emotion was present in the reading.

What emotions did you identify? Why do you consider them emotions? How did you feel? Were they correctly expressed in the story? If the answer is negative, what would have been the best way?

It is necessary that children learn to identify and express emotions correctly from the moment they begin to use reason.

11.– The little theater

Requirements: theater dolls

Number of players: 5 – 10 children

The children will attend their activity with different dolls to participate, the leader will place them in small groups and ask them to do a theatrical performance with their dolls, showing the emotions present in it.

The children will need different dolls for this activity. The leader will place the students in small groups and ask them to do a theatrical performance with their dolls, expressing different emotions with them.

Each group will take turns participating, acting out the emotions but without speaking.

The rest of the class that is observing will have the responsibility of identifying these emotions to discuss them at the end of the presentation.

When everyone has participated, the guide will ask what emotions were presented. Were they handled correctly? Did you identify with any of them?

Participating will help them become familiar with the different emotions and the correct way of expressing them.

12.– We draw

Requirements: sheets, pencils and colors.

Number of players: 5 – 10 children

The leader will give the children paper, pencils and colors, and will indicate that they must draw and color all the emotions that they experience on a daily basis; only drawings, no words.

At the end, they will stand in a circle and present their drawings. Together they will identify each one and give it the correct name.

What emotion is it? Why do you identify it like that? What is the best way to express it? Can you recognize these emotions in yourself?

The activity comes to an end, motivating the children to freely express themselves and to appropriately channel their emotions for an optimal development in their environment.

.

Games to teach empathy

Being empathetic is a valuable trait for a person to have; fostering it from an early age will make them better people and better human beings.

13.- Draw your partner

Requirements: bond paper, pencils and colors

Number of players: 5 - 10 children

The group guide will ask the children to sit in a circle; they will talk about each person's particular characteristics.

Then they will be asked to take their sheet of bond paper and select the partner they want to draw. Once they have drawn it, they will discuss their likes and dislikes, what excites them, what makes them feel fear, happiness, etc.

The guide must ensure that all children actively participate. To end the game, there will be questions and answers to conclude the activity. How did you feel? Did you like how your partner defined you? How do you think your classmates would feel if you did something that they have expressed they like? What have you learned?

The game closes reflecting on the importance of putting ourselves in other peoples' shoes for a better coexistence.

14.- The shoes

Requirements: children's shoes

Number of participants: 5 - 10 children

All the children will sit in a circle, one next to the other. The leader will explain what the activity consists of.

Each of them must remove one shoe. They can either remove their right shoe or their left shoe, but it must be the same side.

Once the shoes are removed, the person on the right side will put on their partner's shoe and initiate a round of questions. Each child will have to answer according to how they consider their partner would answer.

When everyone is done, the guide will open space for each one to share their experience through the following questions: How did you feel? Why do you think it is important to put yourself in the other's shoes? Is it possible to understand your classmates' different opinions?

After that, everyone will elaborate a short reflection on the importance of understanding others and putting themselves in their place.

15.- The cobweb

Requirements: ball of yarn

Number of participants: 5 - 10 children

The game will consist of all the children making a wheel. Starting with the leader, they will take the ball of yarn in their hands, say their name and something they like, and pass the ball to another person while holding on to a string of yarn.

They will do so until everyone has introduced themselves; as the ball of yarn is passed from hand to hand, a huge web will be woven that they will have to work together to unravel.

Due to the knots, it is possible that the objective may not be achieved, but they will learn to be patient and wait for the others to continue.

The activity closes with the following questions: How did the activity make you feel? Do you consider that the actions were too complex? Why is it necessary to work on patience? What did you like the most? What have you learned?

The game ends, expressing the importance of being empathetic with others.

16.– The doll

Requirements: one doll

Number of players: 5 – 10 children

All the children will stand in a circle, and when the guide says to, they will take the doll and make a gesture with it that they wish to express. It can be a smile, a look, a very gentle hair tug or perhaps a pinch.

When they have finished, the leader will indicate that the person on the right will do to the other what the other did to the doll; a kiss, a hug, a pinch, a squeeze. To finish, a space for sharing is opened.

How did you feel? Did you get what you expected? How do you feel about what the other expressed on to you? How should we behave with others?

The dynamic closes with the pertinent reflection on the need to develop empathy in our relationships.

Games to build confidence

Onfidence is necessary in daily life, children need to learn that there are many valuable people, with true affections that are worth trusting, the game becomes an effective tool to transmit this teaching.

17.– Tracked caravans

Requirements: all individuals must participate

Number of players: 5 – 15 children

The group leader will place the children in circles and begin the game by telling a story. The leader will share with the class a walk they took over the weekend, highlighting that while walking through the park in the open air, they had the wonderful opportunity to observe caterpillars.

Then, the children are asked to imagine that they are caterpillars, walking and breathing freely in all the space they are in. As they walk, the leader will explain that caterpillars are great companions and like to walk hand in hand; so they are urged to take a companion by the hand to continue the activity.

After another period of time, they are told that the caterpillars have a lot of trust in each other; so they not only walk hand in hand, but also make a train, one behind the other.

They are told that caterpillars enjoy walking with their eyes closed, so the students are asked to close their eyes and allow themselves to be guided by their companions.

This is how the activity will be carried out until the children have not only found a space for fun, but also for trust.

Finally, a space for questions is given: How did you feel? Were you able to trust your classmates?

The activity closes by emphasizing the need to learn to develop trust.

18.– Guide me

Requirements: all individuals must participate

Number of players: 5 - 15 children

The children will be placed in pairs; the leader will indicate that in order to achieve the objectives, each one will be the other's guide.

Thus, they will be asked to carry out various activities throughout the space: looking for notebooks, drawing a globe, opening the door, moving a chair. Everything must be done with their eyes closed and guided by their classmate.

Everyone should have the opportunity to participate; when they have already achieved several tasks, they are given time to reflect through directed questions.

What did you think of the activity? How did you feel? Did you feel safe being guided by your partner? What have you learned from this experience?

The activity is concluded, giving them the opportunity to share their personal experiences with each other.

19.- Who do you trust?

Requirements: objects and full participation.

Number of players: 5 - 15 children

For this game, each child must have an object of value; this must be requested in advance.

The child will be asked to give the object to someone else whom they trust and consider will take care of it.

In turn, that child will also be given an object which they must take care of until times up. While each student has the object in hand, they can talk to each other, share a common interest, etc..

When the leader indicates, everyone will make a circle to share their experience.

The teacher will proceed to ask them what they thought of the game dynamics. Why did you choose partner X to take care of your object? Why did that person generate more confidence? Did you think your item was safe? Did you feel any fear?

The activity is concluded once everyone has participated and expressed what they have learned.

20.– My goals

Requirements: : class participation, a ball and jump rope

Number of players: 5 - 15 children

Making use of the requirements, each child will set goals to meet.

The guide will explain to the children that they have free time to play, but that each game must end with achieving an objective: The one with the ball will play until they achieve 10 goals, the one with the rope will jump 30 times, and the one with the drum will play for 5 minutes and so on.

The children will be placed into teams of two; one will be in charge of timing while the other does the task. The person timing will indicate when to start and when to stop. Both will have the same task until the guide signals the end of the game. Then they will sit in a circle and begin to discuss what they did.

 How did you feel? Did you feel confident in your partner? Did you think they were going to count wrong? What did you experience? What did you learn?

The leader proceeds to conclude, highlighting the fact that all human beings need to have someone close whom they can trust.

Games to improve self-esteem

Loving yourself is fundamental for the human being, every child must learn love and self-worth from an early age so that they can grow strong in all aspects of life.

21.- The magic jar

Requirements: Glass jar, sheets of paper, pencils

Number of players: 5 - 15 children

The guide will organize the children in a circle where they will share amongst each other their strengths and weaknesses, addressing those areas and situations in which they think their lacking coping skills.

 At the end, they will be given a sheet of paper and pencil, where they must write positive and motivating phrases that they would like to hear and express to others.

Then they will take those phrases and place them in a glass jar, that is, a magic jar.

In the same circle, the guide will take the jar and pass it around; each child will take a phrase and dedicate it to whomever they want, taking into account what the other is lacking.

For example: José, you consider that you don't have the ability to learn quickly; I dedicate this phrase to you: "You can, try one more time."

This is how it will be done child by child, until everyone has a positive phrase to motivate them.

To conclude, the guide will ask how they felt. What do you think of your positive phrase? Why do you think it is important to remember our capabilities? How did it feel to know that your classmate inspired their positive phrase on you? What was the teaching you received?

The game is over when the proposed objective is reached.

22.– The hot seat

Requirements: chairs and class participation

Number of players: 5 - 15 children

The guide will place the children in a circle and in the middle of it a chair, which will be occupied in due course by each student.

Once everyone is located, the leader will ask one of the students to take a seat in the chair, while the rest of the group will begin to circle around them. When the leader says "stop", the child who is in front of the chair will express a positive message towards the student sitting:

"You are very bright", "You are very intelligent", "You are a good classmate", among others. Everyone will have the opportunity to sit in the chair and receive all kinds of positive phrases from the others.

Finally, the guide will ask how they felt. Do you identify with all these expressions? What do you think about self-love? How capable do you consider yourself coping with certain emotions?

The game is concluded, reinforcing the fundamentality of self-worth in each individual.

23.- Positive glasses

Requirements: Imaginary glasses

Number of players: 5 - 15 children

The children will be placed in a circle; the leader will explain that everyone must use their imaginary glasses when instructed.

The leader will begin narrating certain actions, some good others not so much, and at the end will ask the children what they thought of each story. For those actions that have seemed negative, the guide will ask them to put on their magic glasses and visualize something positive.

Once the activity concludes, the leader will explain that many times in life, they will face negative situations where they might feel weak or incapable of managing. In sight of this, they must put on their magic glasses and perceive how all their abilities surpass the limits.

The teacher proceeds to ask the following questions: How did you feel identifying the positive aspects of the action? What things can you do to turn your weaknesses into strengths? Is it necessary to use magic glasses on a day-to-day basis?

After the reflection, a space is opened for sharing and conversing.

24.- The stars

Requirements: stars

Number of players: 5 - 15 children

The children will sit in a circle on the floor; the leader will proceed to explain the game instructions. It will consist of each child saying a motivational word to their partner, while awarding them with a star.

Following a specific order isn't required; more than one child can participate at the same time. If two or three children wish to express their words to the same child, they can do so freely.

When everyone has participated, the activity will close by asking the children how they felt. What did you think of the activity? What do you think of the kind gestures your peers made? How do you identify your strengths and abilities?

Once the game is over, the children will be able to share a little more. This will help them to have greater confidence for the next meeting.

Games to boost intelligence

C hildren are born with an innate intelligence that must be stimulated from an early age; Working on it through play is a practical and attractive way to achieve the goal.

25.- Questions and answers

Requirements: paper and pencil

Number of players: 5 - 15 children

The leader will instruct the children to get into pairs to develop the game. When all are settled, they will proceed to give them a sheet and pencil.

For this game, the leader will instruct the children to form pairs and will hand out a sheet of paper and pencil.

Each pair must choose a topic that is of interest to both, where they will have time to share their experiences and the reasons why they like that topic.

After, the guide will give them a couple of extra minutes to write down some questions with respects to the topic discussed, which must be answered by their partner.

At the end, the pair will debate on the subject using the answers to the specific questions. Then a group discussion will arise to share their experience.

The teacher concludes the activity with directed questions: How did you feel about the activity? What did you think? How did you feel being able to share topics of interest with your peers? What did you learn?

The game is concluded, the children can talk another time with each other, while they are withdrawing from the space.

26.– Memory

Requirements: class participation

Number of players: 5 – 15 children

The game will consist of memorizing names and phrases in order to improve their memory capacity.

The leader will start first by standing up and saying their name along with some personal characteristics. Then, the next person must do the same but also mention the leaders name and the characteristics they said.

This is how the activity will be carried out child by child; even if they don't remember everything, the game must continue until the end.

Once everyone has participated, the leader will proceed to ask: What did you think of the activity? Was it very complex? Did you have a hard time retaining the information? What did you learn?

Finish the game with the answers and a learning strategy that they can use in any other context to help them easily retain information.

27.— Color charts

Requirements: colored cards

Number of players: 5 - 15 children

Children will need different colored cards for this activity, which must be requested in advance. The cards must be of different colors, pink, red, blue, yellow, green, orange, white, black, and as many as they like.

Then in pairs, the leader will indicate them to stand around the table; one of the children will take the cards and place them one by one on the table, mentioning the color out loud, while their other watches and listens attentively.

When the child has finished placing all the cards, the other student who was observing and listening will repeat the colors of the cards that were placed on the table, in the same order that their partner mentioned them.

Then they will change places so that the other child can also have an active participation. In the same way, all the students will have the possibility to participate.

Finally, the leader will ask them to reflect on the activity: What did you think of the game? How did you feel? Was it easy or too complex to remember? Do you think you can remember information quickly? What was the learning acquired?

Once everyone has participated, the game is concluded.

28.- The labyrinth

Requirements: paper, scissors and tape

Number of players: 5 - 15 children

The guide will give the children scissors and paper to cut into four parts. Then they will tape the parts together, making path on the floor to form a labyrinth. It must spread throughout the entire room and in different directions in order to reach the other side. This route will have a starting point and an ending point.

Once this is done, the game will begin. Each child will move from one place to another over the path that has been demarcated. Then that path will be removed and the child will have to move again, from one place to another, but remembering the first route. At the first mistake, they will have to go back and start over. If they make a second mistake, then they lose their turn and it is up to the next person to try. From this second child onwards they have the challenge of remembering the path that was marked with the papers, because by this time it will have already been withdrawn.

Everyone will actively participate and motivate each other to help them remember the way.

The game is concluded under the following questions: What did you think of the activity? Did you find it very difficult to remember the way? How did you feel when you arrived? How did it feel to start over? Were your classmates pleasant when guiding you? What did you learn?

Play time ends and each child leaves the space.

Games to improve gross motor skills

Play activities are great for improving gross motor skills, kids have fun as well as benefit.

29.– Balance and coordination

Requirements: paper foot prints and tape

Number of players: 5 – 15 children

The leader will instruct the children to tape paper footprints on the floor, from one end to the other in the space in which they are in, indicating a starting and ending point.

Then the leader will explain that, one by one, each student will follow the prints throughout the entire space from beginning to end. However, they must be attentive to the instructions given by their guide as they pass; they may be asked to stop and lift their right or left leg for a few seconds. If they fail to maintain it, they must return to the starting point and wait for a new turn. This will be done successively, so that all the students have the opportunity to actively participate.

Once everyone has gone, the game ends with the following questions: What did you think of the game? How did you feel? Was the path too complex? What motivated you to try again when you made a mistake? What was the learning obtained?

The children will be able to share a little more afterwards and then leave the space.

30.- The wheelbarrow

Requirements: plastic cones

Number of players: 5 - 15 children

All the children will randomly pick a partner, while the guide places the cones indicating the starting and ending point.

When all the space is completely arranged, they will begin to play wheelbarrow.

One of the partners will be placed on the floor, face down, while the other takes them by the feet. The child who is on the floor will start walking on their hands, while their partner guides them.

Once they reach the finish line, they must go back to the starting point and start again, but this time the roles will have changed, one on the floor and the other holding them by the feet.

They can repeat the activity as many times as the leader indicates, in fact, they can also change partners.

Afterwards, everyone will sit in a circle and the game will conclude by answering the following questions: How did you feel? Were you able to work together as a team? What values did you put into practice? Do you like physical activity? What did you learn from the game?

31.- Bowling

Requirements: bottles filled with sand and a ball.

Number of participants: 5 - 15 children

The leader will demarcate the space in which the game will take place. They will make a vertical line where at one end the bowling pins will be placed horizontally and at the other the children will be standing.

The game begins; one by one, each child will throw the ball to try and knock down all the pins. For this, they must coordinate the exact movements so that they can hit the target.

The leader will indicate how many chances they will get; everyone will have the opportunity to participate as many times as their guide allows them, until they achieve the task.

The game ends with directed questions: What did you think of the game? Did you have fun? What did you learn from the activity? How did it feel to achieve the goal? How did you feel when you missed? How important do you think physical activity is?

32.– Aiming colors

Requirements: colored baskets and balls

Number of players: 5 – 15 children

Children should bring colored baskets and balls for this activity; these must be requested in advance.

The children will make a circle and in the center of it they will place a basket. At the command of their guide, they will each try and throw the ball in the basket. They must do their best to get as many as possible.

The game is followed by a few questions regarding the activity. What did you think of the game? How did you feel participating? How complex did it seem? Did you learn anything new? What do you think of your classmates' participation?

After the reflection, the children will be able to continue with a recreational space before leaving.

Games to develop patience

Patience is an essential virtue needed when facing many situations in our lives.

33.- The egg race

Requirements: eggs and teaspoons

Number of players: 5 - 15 children

The guide will ask the children in advance to bring an egg and a spoon for the following game; everyone will participate.

A line will be drawn on the floor with a starting point and an ending point.

Then the students will be grouped into teams of 4; they must take the spoon and place it in their mouth with an egg on the tip of it.

At the voice of the leader, they will start the race; the goal is to reach the finish line without dropping the egg. They must reach the end, turn around and return to the starting point.

The activity will be carried out as many times as necessary so that they can acquire greater skill.

After the game is over, a space will open for sharing. What did you think of the game? How did you feel during the race? What was the challenge? What did you find more complex? What did you learn from the activity?

34.- Ring toss

Requirements: wooden sticks, small rings and a few pots with dirt.

Number of players: 5 - 15 children

The leader must indicate to the children that for the next meeting they will have to bring wooden sticks and small rings.

For this game, the students will stand in a circle and the guide will place the pots in the center with a wooden stick buried in each of them.

The game will consist of each child tossing the rings in order to land it around the stick.

The activity will be repeated as many times as the leader indicates so that the children can fully participate.

It is not about who manages to score the most rings, but who has the most patience in achieving the task.

The activity closes with the following questions: How did you feel trying to achieve the objective? Did it seem very complex? What did you think of your classmates' participation? Who were the most patient? What did you learn from this activity?

This game focuses on developing patience in order to overcome adversity.

35.– Complete the sentence

Requirements: a story

Number of players: 5 - 15 children

The children will sit in a circle, one next to the other; the leader will start by reading a fun and entertaining story. While reading, the guide will make several pauses during which the children must, in an orderly manner and when granted by the guide, intervene and share the phrase that they consider is missing. The phrase chosen must give meaning to the fragment of the story.

It is possible that the phrase may or may not be correct; when it is the case that they do not get it right, the leader will start the story over again under the same dynamics. The reading will only continue when the phrase indicated by the children is the most appropriate and make sense.

Once the narration is finished, the leader will proceed to ask what they thought of the activity. How did you feel about your participation? How did it feel to find the correct phrase? What did you feel when you were wrong and we had to start all over? What did you learn from this activity?

The activity ends by reinforcing the importance of developing patience in order to achieve the proposed objectives.

36.– Color the image

Requirements: paper and colors

Number of players: 5 – 15 children

The guide will proceed to give each child a sheet of paper with an image on it; it can be an animal, a flower, or any other object. The students will be requested in advance to bring the same shades of colors for this activity.

The activity will consist of each child painting their drawing; however, the guide will indicate the different colors that the students will be using. The game must be well timed, so that when the guide requests the color change everyone is ready. This will require both patience and concentration.

After the activity, the children will reflect through directed questions: Which part of the activity did you enjoy the most? Which part was the most complex? How did you feel? Did you feel rushed to finish before the guide indicated the color change? What did you learn?

The game ends by emphasizing the importance of developing patience, a virtue present in everyday life.

Games to
develop self-control

Many times children tend to be explosive, it is necessary for them to learn self-control to avoid future conflicts.

37.– The guide

Requirements: handkerchiefs

Number of players: 5 – 15 children

The children will be divided into two groups, one group will be blindfolded and the other will be able to see.

The leader will instruct the children who are blindfolded, to choose a person to guide them around the room. They will have to walk and select their guide without being able to see them.

The guide selected will start the tour, indicating the person who can't see where to walk and where not to. It is possible that the person being guided will want to choose the way, however, the guide will be the only one to carry out this task.

At the voice of the teacher, everyone will stop, exchange roles and repeat the activity; this way everyone can participate.

The game ends with the following questions: What did you think of the game? How did you feel? Were you comfortable? Were you tempted to take over and choose the way? Do you feel like your guide led at all times? What did you learn?

The activity is concluded, opening a space for the children to share their experience.

38.– Simon says

Requirements: different objects

Number of children: 5 - 15 children

The children will be placed in a circle and among all they will choose who will play the role of Simon.

The game will consist of Simon dividing the students in small groups and giving them instructions to follow. One group will start first. When Simon says an action, the students must do as they are told, but only when he starts the phrase with "Simon says..."For example "Simon says to sing a song", "Simon says to say the alphabet", etc. The children must respond to Simon's requests, however, if the person doesn't say "Simon says" first, then they must stay still and not move.

Successively, the groups will change until everyone has participated. The game will end with the following questions: What did you think of the activity? Which part was the most fun? What did you think of Simon's requests? Was it difficult to follow directions? What lesson did the game teach you?

39.– The frozen dance

Requirements: music

Number of players: 5 – 15 children

The leader will begin by explain the game rules; everyone will be standing in a circle.

The guide will start playing music and the children will dance, either in a group, in pairs or alone. When the music stops, they too must stop, when the music continues, they must continue; whoever fails to freeze when the music stops will be disqualified. The game will continue until only one person remains standing.

If everyone manages to keep the rhythm between dancing and freezing, then everyone will be a winner.

The game ends with directed questions: What did you think of the activity? Did you like dancing? Did you find it difficult to follow directions? How did you perceive your peers during the game? What did you learn?

After the reflection, all the children will be able to leave.

40.– 1, 2, 3 English chick

Requirements: children

Number of players: 5 – 15 children

The teacher will explain to the children what the game consists of; among all, they will choose a child who will be the English chick.

The child who plays the chick will stand at one end of the room and the rest of the children will stand at the other end, one next to the other.

The baby chick, facing the wall, will start the count, "1, 2, 3 English chicks". While counting, the children will walk towards the chick until they say "English chick", in which the chick will then turn around and the children will have to stay still. Anyone who does not freeze and is caught moving will be disqualified. This will be done successively, until the majority is eliminated and one or two people remain.

Space for reflection opens up. What did you think of the game? Did you enjoy it? What did you think of the chick's participation? Was it difficult for you to stop and stay still? Would you like to play again? What lesson did the game teach you?

The children can continue playing a while longer, and then leave the space.

Games to develop creativity

E very child has a creative side; all they need is a little push to let their imagination run wild.

41.– Draw and paint

Requirements: sheet of paper, colors, and a story

Number of players: 5 - 15 children

The leader will explain the rules of the game and hand out sheets of paper; the children must already have their colors in hand.

The guide will begin by telling a very dynamic and fun story. While speaking, the children will imagine the story and begin to draw what the story has inspired them.

At the end, each child will color their drawing and share it with the rest of the class, showcasing their creativity.

Conclude the activity with directed questions: How did you feel while listening? How inspired were you to draw? How do you feel about your creation? What do you think of your classmates' creativity? Did it seem very complex? What did you learn from the game?

Time is up and everyone proceeds to withdraw from the space.

42.- Create a story

Requirements: papers and pencils

Number of players: 5 - 15 children

The leader will organize the children in pairs; each will be given a sheet of paper and a pencil.

They will then be instructed to select a topic that they both like and will be given plenty of time to share ideas. After that, they will create a story based on what each expressed they like. Both students must participate with their ideas so that they can complement each other.

When they have finished, each pair will have the opportunity to read their stories to the rest of the group.

End the activity with a space for reflection. How did you feel creating a story of your favorite topic? Did you like working with someone else? What was it like to discover you had common interests with your partner? Did you like the idea of creating something? What do you think of your partner's creativity? What was the lesson learned?

The game is over and they say goodbye until the next meeting.

43.– What word is next?

Requirements: class participation

Number of players: 5 – 15 children

The leader will place the children in a circle; they will sit next to each other, attentive to the directions given to them.

The guide will begin by saying a phrase and the child sitting next to them must complete it. Example: the guide will say "Charles is studious", and the person next to them will complete the sentence by adding "...and he likes dancing...", and the next child will add "...and singing".

In this manner, everyone will participate until the last person in the circle plays. After that, they can start over with another name and other ideas, until the leader concludes the game and opens the space for reflection.

How did you feel about the game? Did you find it difficult? What do you think of the added phrases? Which part was the funniest? Do you think that you can be more creative? What did you learn from the game?

44.– What is it called?

Requirements: paper and pencil

Number of players: 5 – 15 children

The group leader will give the children a sheet of paper and pencil to carry out the activity.

The game will consist of the leader telling a funny story, but there will be no specific characters or details of the environment, colors, objects, etc. The children must listen carefully from beginning to end.

Once the reading is finished, they will have the task of shaping the story and giving it a title. They must create characters, names, environments, and everything they want to highlight in the story. Then, they will read their stories to the rest of group.

To conclude, the guide will ask the following questions: What did you think of the story? What made you think of those missing details? What inspired your creation? What do you think of your classmates' creations? What did you learn from the game?

The activity ends with everyone sharing their experience.

Conflict Resolution games

Conflicts appear in daily life; acquiring tools to handle them is essential from an early age, in order to overcome obstacles and achieve goals.

45.- The circle

Requirements: full participation

Number of players: 5 - 15 children

The children will form a circle, and then a group of about six children will form a smaller circle within the group, that is, in the center.

The students will then choose a current topic that is of interest to them to discuss the conflict it presents. The group that is in the center will have the task of debating and looking for possible solutions according to the case. Once they have reached an agreement, they will proceed to discuss the solution with the rest of the group surrounding them. They will then debate amongst each other, whether it is the best solution to the conflict.

The activity can be repeated as many times as the leader indicates; the groups in the center can be rotated.

At the end, a space for reflection will be opened: How did you feel during the activity? What did you think of the conflict? What did you think of the solution? What did you think of your classmates' different contributions? Do you think that the chosen solution was the correct one? If there had been room for another solution, which one would you have chosen? What did you learn from this activity?

46.– The spider web

Requirements: rope

Number of players: 5 – 15 children

With the help of the guide, the children form a spider web, passing the rope wherever there is an open space but leaving small free spaces. When it is completely woven, the game can begin.

One by one, the students will have to make use of the free spaces, going through the cobweb but without touching the rope. If at any time it seems complex, they will have to find a solution to their conflict.

When everyone has passed, they will stand in a circle for a short reflection. How did you feel about the activity? Which part seemed the most difficult? Was it difficult for you to find a solution? What did you learn from the game?

The children say goodbye until the next meeting, teaching them the importance of seeking assertive responses to daily conflicts.

47.– The dramatization

Requirements: children

Number of players: 5 – 15 children

The children will sit in a circle and create different stories, real or imaginary, to then act out.

Then they will be divided into small groups of 5, where each group will choose a story to present. They will be given a few minutes to prepare. These stories must present a conflict and a solution; it may be based on their family, their community or their school.

When everyone has participated, they will share and study the different solutions presented, expressing whether there were other ways of dealing with the conflict.

The game ends with directed questions: What did you think of the game? How did you feel dramatizing the stories? Do you think there could have been more than one solution? What do you think of your classmates' contributions? What was the learning acquired?

This concludes the game in its entirety.

48.– What would you do?

Requirements: class participation

Number of players: 5 – 15 children

The children will sit in a circle and share amongst each other a situation that happened to them and that they consider was a real problem. Then they must come up with a solution to resolve it.

One by one, each child will present a problem and a solution, and the person on the right must provide a different solution to that proposed by the child speaking. This will be done successively until everyone has participated.

The game closes with a short reflection, answering the following questions: What did you think of the activity? How did you feel when telling your story? What did you think of the different solutions presented? What did you learn from this game?

After sharing their experiences, the students can leave the space.

Games to develop critical thinking skills

C ritical thinking skills are necessary in order to respond to daily demands and arrive at the best possible solutions for them, thus avoiding frustrations.

49.– Why?

Requirements: full participation

Number of players: 5 – 15 children

For this game, a small group of students will be selected, it can be 4 or 5, and the leader will present them with a topic of their liking. Then, that group will leave the room while the teacher gives the rest of the class instructions. Everyone must listen carefully to what the children outside are going to expose. Once they are done talking, they will raise their hands and ask a question, which will always be "why?"

One by one, each child will enter the room and present their topic. Then, someone from the class will raise their hand and ask the question, "why?" This will be done successively, until the child who is speaking notices that it is a joke. The person will then take a seat on the floor with the rest of the class, while the next person enters the room to present.

Once everyone from that group has presented, the game concludes and a space for reflection is opened.

How did you feel about the game? What did you think? When your classmates asked "why", did you know it was a joke? What can you improve? What have you learned today?

Finish the game by emphasizing the importance of developing critical thinking skills. In everyday situations, they will find a "why" and must be able to give it a timely answer..

50.- Questions and answers

Requirements: a bell

Number of players: 5 - 15 children.

The leader will demarcate the space for the game to be played. It will have a starting point and an end point where there will be a table and a bell.

The game will consist of questions and answers. Together the class will choose a current and attractive topic that everyone knows; it can be about values, culture, fashion, cuisine, sports, among others. The leader will then draw up a list of questions regarding the chosen topic.

 At the starting point, children will be standing in 4 rows of 4. The guide will be at the other end with the list of questions. Following the first question, the first child in each row who knows the answer, will run towards the table where the bell is, ring it and give their response. In the same way, it will be done with the rest of the children until the game ends.

After the activity, the teacher will ask following questions: Did you enjoy playing the game? Who wanted to get there first? What did you think of the race? What did you think of your classmates' answers? Did everyone agree? What was the learning obtained?

Play time ends and each child can leave.

51.- Follow the track

Requirements: different objects, paper and pencil

Number of participants: 5 - 15 children

Requirements: different objects, paper and pencil.

Number of participants: 5 - 15 children.

For this activity, the children will need different objects that the leader will ask for in advance; they will be divided into small groups of 4.

The leader will take paper and pencil and write down clues according to the different objects. The children will exit the room for a few minutes, while the guide hides the clues and objects in strategic places.

Then, the children will reenter the space and start the game. They will start off with one clue that will lead them to a hidden object and another clue. They will continue looking for clues until they have found all the hidden objects, thus ending the game.

There is room for reflection through the following questions: How did you feel during the game? What did you think of it? Was it fun? Did you encounter any difficulties? Were you able to work together and get the job done? What did you learn?

52.– Who tells the truth?

Requirements: the class will be divided into groups

Number of players: 5 - 15 children

The children will sit in a circle and the leader will explain the game. A group of students will be selected by their peers to come forward and tell a comedy or a tragedy; this can be inspired by true or fictional events. The rest of the group will listen carefully. When each student has finished telling their story, the leader will proceed to ask "who is telling the truth?"

The children who are seated must answer which of the interpreted actions is real and which is not. The child who answers incorrectly must stand in the front and create a new story that the rest must evaluate and determine if it's true or false.

This will be done successively until everyone has had the opportunity to participate. The game ends with the following questions: What did you think of the game? What did you experience? What did you think of your classmates' participation? Was it difficult to identify which actions were real and which were not? How can you distinguish between real and fake? What was the learning obtained?

The activity is focused on developing critical thinking skills from a young age.

Anger Management games

Anger is an emotion that, if not controlled from a very young age, can generate great internal and external conflicts. Learning to manage this emotion will help the child address and resolve situations with a clear mind and in a healthy manner.

53.- The Anger Bomb

Requirements: a paper bag, sheets of paper and pencils

Number of children: 5 - 15 children

The leader will begin the activity by talking to the students about anger and self-control. Then, the leader will explain the different strategies and tools that they can use to cope with difficult situations. Among these, they will put into practice the game "ticking time bomb"; since anger is like a bomb that if not externalized, can explode inside, hurting not only the person but everyone around them.

With this activity they will learn how to deactivate their anger.

The children will be placed into groups of 2 or 3. For this task, each will need paper and pencil; they must think and write the necessary steps to defuse their anger bomb. Example: stay calm, breathe deeply, think about what triggered the bomb, talk with someone, etc. Then they will put the sheets of paper in their paper bags.

Once everyone has finished, they will sit forming a circle, and place the bags in the center.

When the leader says "the bomb has been activated", all the students will get up and run towards the center. The first person to arrive will grab a bag and quickly return to the circle. They will take out the piece of paper and follow the written suggestions on how to deactivate the bomb.

This will be done as many times as the leader indicates, until they are able to put into practice all the tools and strategies that they have learned. This way, when facing situations of anger they will remember that there are many ways to deactivate the bomb.

The game closes with the following questions: What did you think of the activity? How did you feel? How can you relate the game to real life? Is it necessary to defuse the bomb in time? What do you think of the different ways to defuse an anger bomb? What did you learn from this experience?

54.- The balloon and the anger

Requirements: balloons, paper and pencils

Number of players: 5 - 15 children

The children will sit in a circle with their leader to talk about the meaning of anger and the different ways that exist to control it.

For this activity, they will write a situation or situations that make them feel anger. Then, they will take the piece of paper, place it inside a balloon, and proceed to inflate it. When everyone has finished, they will go outside and at the voice of their guide, will release the balloons into the air. After that, they will return to the classroom and sit back down.

The teacher will explain that when facing tough situations, the best solution is to simply take a deep breath and let go of the anger inside, just like a balloon flying away. This exercise will guarantee peace of mind.

The game ends with the following questions: How do you feel? What did you think of the game? What should be done in situations that make you angry? How did you feel when you saw your balloon flying away? Why is it important to channel anger correctly? What was the learning obtained?

The activity is concluded, everyone can leave the space.

55.– Simulating the flame of anger

Requirements: class participation

Number of players: 5 - 15 children

The children and their leader will sit in a circle, so that he or she can explain the rules of the game.

The students will first be divided into small groups; each one will have to act out a different scenario, in a park, in a car, at the beach, at school, etc, in which a fire breaks out and they have to try and find different strategies to put out the flames, either using a water hose, a bucket, a fire extinguisher, or simply running away.

Everyone will have the chance to participate until the game is over. At the end, there will be a space for reflection.

What did you think of the activity? How did you feel during the activity? How do you feel now? Why do you think that was the best way to put out the fire? What did you think of your classmates' strategies? How else would it have been possible to put out the flames? Why did the flames have to be put out on time? What did you learn from the game?

This activity helps the students to understand that the fire represents their anger, which if not extinguished on time can lead to serious problems.

56.– Don't say it

Requirements: colored card

Number of players: 5 – 15 children

All the children will sit in a circle with their guide, conversing about anger and the things that trigger it.

Then the leader will take the colored cards, which they will have brought beforehand, and explain that all the colors represent freedom, except for the black card which means "don't say it". Therefore, if the leader shows them the black card, the child who is speaking must be silent.

Once the activity starts, the students will begin talking again but this time the conversation will become deeper and more detailed; what is it that really bothers them so much that they explode? Why and how do they explode? That is, how do they act or what do they say? What do they express?

The children will voluntarily begin to participate. The leader will hold the cards and little by little will lift them up, letting everyone see them. The child speaking must keep his gaze fixed on the cards. When the leader perceives that the child is expressing an action or word that is not correct for proper anger management, they will hold up the black card and the child will have to be silent. They must take a deep breath and continue speaking until they are done.

The card can be shown as many times as necessary; all children will have the opportunity to actively participate until the game is finished.

The teacher will proceed to ask the following questions: What did you think of the game? How did you feel while participating? How do you feel now? What did you think of using the colored cards for self-control? What was the learning acquired?

Time is up and everyone leaves the space until the next opportunity to share.

Resilience building games

The world and its great advances can be overwhelming for some; because of this, resilience must be fostered in children so they can learn to face whichever situation may come their way.

57.- The mirror

Requirements: sheets of bond paper, pencils and colors

Number of players: 5 - 15 children

The leader will explain the instructions that the students must follow in order to carry out the activity. They will have to tape several sheets of bond paper together to make one big piece of paper, that way several children will be able to participate. Once that's done, they will sit in a circle and place the big sheet of paper in the center, along with the pencils and colors.

Two students will be selected or will volunteer to stand in the middle of the circle. One will lay facing up on the large sheet of paper, while the other will draw out their silhouette. Then, the one being drawn will get up so that their partner can finish the details; eyes, eyelashes, mouth, nose, and ears. When finished, the child will lay back down over their silhouette.

The rest of the students will then write down on the same paper a characteristic and positive word describing that child.

Once everyone has finished writing, the child will get up and read what was written about them. Then, they will take their place and allow another two students to participate.

The activity will be carried out as many times as the leader indicates, leaving space at the end for reflection: What did you think of the activity? How did you feel? How do you feel about the words describing you? Can you identify your strengths? What did you learn from the game?

The activity concludes and the children leave the place until the next meeting.

58.– The toolbox

Requirements: shoe box, pencils, paper sheets, colors

Number of children: 5 – 15 children

The leader will hand out paper and pencils; the students must have the shoe box and the colors requested beforehand.

Before starting the game, the leader will explain that they are going to design a toolbox, reminding them of its usefulness when there is a problem to solve. The difference will be that, in this box, the tools will be exclusively to face difficult situations present on a daily basis. It will not be a hammer, a nail or a screw, instead it will be patience, tolerance, respect, empathy; each one will be represented with a different color.

The teacher will give them a reasonable amount of time to carry out the activity. At the end, they will have the opportunity to open their toolbox and share with the rest of the class the tools that they have created, as well as the situation in which they will be used. Example: my green patience will help me when I have to study for an exam, my blue tolerance will help me when the people in my book club have a different opinion from mine, my yellow empathy...

In this way, the activity will be conducted until the game ends. Then a space for reflection will be opened.

What did you think of the game? What do you think of your toolbox? Do you think it is useful? What do you think of the other toolboxes? Was it very difficult to identify the tools you need? What was the learning acquired?

After the activity, they say goodbye and leave the space.

59.- Raised hands

Requirements: full participation

Number of players: 5 - 15 children

The children will sit in a circle until the leader tells them to stand up. When indicated, they will begin to make a series of movements as directed by the teacher; hands up, hands down, hand on foot, right foot forward and so on. The only exception will be that when the teacher say "hands up", they will have to keep their hands up in the air until they are told otherwise. This will measure their resistance. No one can lower their arms before the order is given. If someone drops one or both hands, the person on each side will have the task of helping them raise their arms back up until the leader indicates the next move.

 This is how they will carry out the dynamics until the activity is over.

Then, the students will sit back down in a circle and answer the following questions: What did you think of the game? Did you like it? How did you feel during the game? Did you feel tired? How did it feel to get help from your peers? Would you have done the same for them? What do you think of your capabilities? What was the learning obtained?

The day concludes teaching the children that every human being has the capacity to be resilient in the face of adverse situations, all they need are the tools to address them and overcome them.
Time ends, guaranteeing the children the desired learning, every human being has the capacity to be resilient in the face of adverse

situations that arise on a day-to-day basis, you just have to have and use the necessary tools to address them and leave strengthened, which better time to learn from it, than since childhood.

60.- Repeat the tongue twister

Requirements: class participation

Number of players: 5 - 15 children

The children will sit in a circle with their leader, who will explain the game.

The game will consist of repeating several tongue twisters; the guide will have a list and each child will be able to choose which one they want to repeat.

Tongue twisters are generally very complex phrases that require a lot of effort. For this reason, the child may find it necessary to make more than one attempt to achieve the goal.

 One student will say the phrase, while the other children can help by suggesting ways to succeed in the attempt.

Once each child has had their turn, the game will close with a reflection. What did you think of the game? How did you feel? Did you make a great effort to repeat the phrase? What do you think of your classmates' suggestions? Did you think you weren't going to be able to accomplish saying it? What was the learning obtained?

Games to promote sharing

Although children love playing with others, many times they find it difficult to share their toys and belongings. The games in this chapter have the intention of promoting these healthy habits in order to improve their interpersonal relationships.

61.– Create images

Requirements: scissors, paper sheets, pencils, colors

Number of players: 5 – 15 children

The children will sit in pairs while the leader explains the instructions and hands out the materials for the game. They will receive a sheet of paper, pencils, scissors and colors. The activity will consist in creating several images, drawing them, coloring them and cutting them out.

Each pair will have the necessary materials to work with but will have to share and take turns using them.

When everyone has finished, they will stand in front of their classmates and share their experience.

The activity will end with the following directed questions: How did you feel during the activity? How did it feel working with few materials? How do you feel now? Were you able to work together as a team? How was your experience sharing the materials? What did you learn?

62.– The fruit game

Requirements: fruits

Number of players: 5 – 15 children

The children will be requested to bring their favorite fruits for this activity. Everyone will sit in a circle and the leader will explain the rules of the game.

The activity will consist of each child standing up and exchanging fruits with another person. One by one, they will do this until everyone has exchanged fruits. When finished, a space for reflection will open.

What did you think of the activity? How did you feel sharing? Do you like the fruit that was given to you? Why should we share? What was the learning obtained?

The games ends and the students proceed to leave the place.

63.- In search of treasure

Requirements: different objects

Number of players: 5 - 15 children

The children will be divided into small groups and the teacher will proceed to explain the rules of the treasure hunt.

The first thing the children must do is to withdraw a few minutes from the space, while the leader hides the different objects in strategic places. Once all the objects have been hidden, the children will reenter the space to begin the quest, during which they must share the different tools available to them to carry out the task; shovels, scissors, rope, among others. Since the children will be looking for treasure, they must pretend that they are in the jungle or a similar space.

When they have finished finding all the objects, the game will conclude to give space for reflection.

What did you think of the activity? How did you feel? Was it very complex to find the treasure? How was your experience working together with your classmates? Were the tools you used sufficient? What was the learning acquired?

The activity ends and they leave the place.

64.- Yours and mine

Requirements: different objects.

Number of players: 5 - 15 children

The students will need different objects for this activity, which will be requested in advance.

First, the leader will place them in pairs and give them free time to play. Then, the students will be able to choose a game of their liking, with the exception that they will have to exchange with each other the different objects that they brought. They will all carry out the activity by playing with their classmates' objects.

This is how time will pass until the leader indicates that the game is over, and opens a space for reflection.

What game did you play? How did you feel? Did you like sharing your objects? What did you think of playing with someone else's object? How do you feel now? Why is sharing important? What did you learn from this activity?

The activity concludes and with it they proceed to leave the place until the next meeting.

Exploring identity games

It is important for children to explore their identity from an early age, this way they will be able to adequately carry out their role in society. These games represent an effective way to accomplish this objective.

65.- The mirror game

Requirements: class participation

Number of players: 5 - 15 children

The children will be divided into pairs; one child will stand in front of the other as if they were a mirror. They will begin by making a series of expressions, which must be imitated by their partner who is observing them.

Then, the pair will start a conversation describing who they are, what they like, how they define themselves, etc. The leader may request that they switch partners and repeat the activity.

Finally, a space is opened for reflection. What did you think of the game? How did you feel? How would you describe yourself? What do you think of your classmate? How would you define them in one word? What did you learn from the activity?

The activity ends with the children sharing their experience.

.

66.- Draw what is missing

Requirements: bond, paper, pencils and tape.

Number of players: 5 - 15 children.

The children will be placed in pairs by their leader, who in turn will give them several sheets of bond paper, tape, and pencils.

The first thing they will do is to take several sheets of bond paper and join them together with tape, making two large flip charts. Then they will proceed to draw each other, making it as detailed as possible. When the drawings are finished, they will talk about what they believe is missing from their portraits; perhaps more hair, a smile, slightly smaller eyes, among others.

Then, they will add the person's name and characteristics describing them. Example: "My name is Luis". "I am intelligent, playful, studious..."

At the end, they will share their creations with the rest of their classmates and will close with a little reflection. What did you think of the activity? How did you feel? How do you feel now? What did you think of your classmates' drawings? Were many traits or characteristics missing? How were you defined? What did you learn?

67.– Tell your story

Requirements: an object of value

Number of players: 5 - 15 children

Children should bring to the meeting place an object that is of their liking and of great value to them.

The leader will sit them in a circle, and with their object in hand, they will receive the instructions to start the activity. It will consist of creating a story of their object, narrating the reasons why it's so important to them. At the end, the person sitting at the right of the child who is speaking will add a characteristic that they consider define the child in question.

Once everyone has participated, the leader will take the floor and ask the following questions: How were you defined? Why is it important to know who we are, to know our identity? How did you feel during the activity? Do you think our interests define us? What do you think of the way each person defines themselves? What did you learn from the game?

The activity comes to an end and the students leave the space.

68.- Look for the chair

Requirements: chairs, paper sheets, paper, markers, plastic tape, handkerchief, music

Number of players: 5 - 15 children

When the leader indicates, the children will take paper and write their name on it with marker, then tape it on a chair.

In a circle, each student will take their handkerchief and cover their eyes. The leader will begin to play music, and with their eyes covered, the students will slowly start walking around the room so as not to bump into each other. When the music stops, they must stop, remove their scarf and look for the chair with their name on it to sit down. The leader will choose a few students at random and ask why they sat on that chair. Each child must answer that the chair had their name on it, therefore corresponding to them.

The children will once again cover their eyes and the leader will move the chairs around to repeat the game.

After the activity, there will be a time for reflection. How did you feel? What did you think of the activity? Why should we be able to identify ourselves? What did you think of the game? Did you learn anything new?

The games ends and everyone can leave.

Teambuilding games

Teamwork is necessary in almost all human environments; learning this from an early age provides students with fundamental tools to improve group performance.

69.- Tug of war

Requirements: rope

Number of players: 5 - 15 children

The leader will sit the children in a circle and explain the rules of the game.

The students will be divided into two teams where they will have to pretend that they are on a sinking boat. The leader will draw a line on the floor dividing the two teams, one on each side.

The children will have the responsibility of not letting the boat sink by playing tug of war; each team will be on opposite ends of the rope and will have to try and pull the other team over the line. The team that pulls the hardest and drags the other across the line wins, thus saving the boat.

The activity can be repeated as many times as the leader indicates, so that everyone can feel like winners and saviors.

Once the activity has been completed, the teacher will ask the following questions: What did you think of the activity? How did you feel? How did you feel about preventing the ship from sinking? Why was everyone's participation so important? Do you think that individually you could have saved the ship? What was the learning obtained?

Finally the game is concluded, until the next meeting.

70.– The earthquake

Requirements: children

Number of players: 5 – 15 children

The guide will sit the children in a circle to explain how the game will develop.

It will consist of working as a team so that the earthquake does not wreak havoc, everyone will begin to walk freely through space, at the voice of the "earthquake" leader, everyone will begin to tremble.

As they will be simulating the action, when the leader indicates that the earthquake has ended, everyone will stand in a circle and begin to give contributions to repair the damage caused, how to raise fallen walls, demolished houses, trapped people, among others.

The idea is that, with the contributions of each one, the conversation is enriched and as a team they define a complete restructuring plan.

At the end of their participation, there will be room for reflection, What did you feel when simulating an earthquake? Do you think that the contributions of each one are useful for the restructuring? Would it be possible to restore the damage caused by the earthquake by working individually? What is the importance of teamwork? What did they learn from the game?

After the reflection, the game time is dismissed.

71.– Tethered

Requirements: class participation

Number of players: 5 – 15 children

The leader will explain the rules of the game, and divide the students into pairs. The children will have to carry out a series of actions but tied together by their show laces; a right shoe with a left shoe or vice versa.

 For example, write on the board, look for a chair, hug someone, sit down, get up, etc. Each activity will be done together as a pair. If they believe that they will not be able to carry out the action, they will have to seek help from another couple, but will also have to tie themselves to their shoes.

In this way, the game will take place until everyone has achieved their task. The activity will conclude with a space for reflection.

What did you think of the game? How did you feel being tied to your partner? Did you find teamwork difficult or was it easy? Did they need more help? What was the learning obtained?

72.- Take the ball

Requirements: a ball

Number of players: 5 - 15 children

The students will be placed in pairs and have the task of moving the ball from one place to another, but without using their hands. They will talk amongst each other to come up with a plan to achieve the objective.

The game begins; the leader will mark the space, indicating a starting point and an ending point. Each pair will take their ball however they see fit, between foot and foot, against each other's backs, between arms, etc, but without touching it with their hands.

The first to reach the finish line wins, while the rest will continue playing until the last couple finishes.

A space for reflection opens. What did you think of the game? How did you feel carrying out the task as a team? Did you find it complex? Did you enjoy it? What are the benefits of teamwork? What did you learn?

The activity ends and they proceed to leave the place.

.

Games to improve concentration and focus

All the tasks simple or complex, require concentration; developing it from an early age will allow the child to approach problems more efficiently.

73.— Follow the clock hands

Requirements: class participation

Number of players: 5 - 15 children

Standing in a circle, the children will begin with a calm breathing exercise directed by their leader, so that they can achieve the objective of the game.

When they are ready, the class will be divided into two. They will form a circle, facing one another, that is, one group outside and the other inside the circle. When the leader indicates, they will begin to turn clockwise towards the time established, first those outside the circle and then those inside. They must be very attentive to when the leader indicates change.

The activity will be repeated as many times as the leader desires and then will close with a space for reflection.

What did you think of the game? How did you feel? Was there a lot of chaos? Was it hard to concentrate? Why do you think it is important to be attentive to our surroundings? Explain what you learned.

The activity ends and everyone leaves the place.

74.– Identify the sound

Requirements: different objects

Number of players: 5 – 15 children

The children will sit in a circle and listen to the guidelines of the game. They will take the different objects that they brought and place them in the center for when they need to be used

The game will consist of the leader picking up the objects one by one and making various sounds. The children will have their eyes closed; when the leader makes the sound corresponding to an object, a child will be selected to identify which sound it is. Each person will be asked to listen carefully in order to give the correct answer.

The game comes to an end with the following questions: What did you think of the activity? How did you feel? Did you find it difficult to identify the sounds? Was it easy to concentrate? Is concentrating a necessary task? What did you learn?

Before leaving the space, it is important to reinforce the concept of concentration because it will allow them to accomplish great things in their lives.

75.—Look similarities and differences

Requirements: objects, drawings and images

Number of players: 5 - 15 children

The children must bring the required elements that the leader will request in advance. They will be divided into small groups and will work with the drawings, objects and images that each one brought.

The activity will consist in observing each of the required elements and finding their similarities and differences, that is, which are those things that make them the same and which are those that make them different.

The leader will give them a few minutes and once they have finished, they will share their experience with the group.

The activity ends with a small reflection. What did you think of the activity? How did you feel? Was the task very complex? Did you need concentration to achieve the goal? What did you learn?

The time is up and they leave the place until the next meeting.

76.– Draw the picture

Requirements: paper, pencils and colors

Number of players: 5 – 15 children

The leader will explain the instructions and pass out paper, pencils and colors, so that the students can carry out the activity.

The leader will begin by drawing an object on the blackboard; the children must carefully observe how the leader does it and then reproduce it on their paper.

Once the leader has finished, the children will proceed to draw the picture on their sheet of paper and color it. For this, they must remain concentrated since the objective is to make the image as precise as possible.

At the end, they will share their drawings with the rest of the class and a space will be opened for reflection. What did you think of the activity? Was it easy to replicate the drawing? How did you feel? Are you happy with your results? What did you learn?

Games to develop discipline in children

For many children, being disciplined is not an easy task but it is an ability that will help them to stay motivated, work hard and excel in life.

77.- Frozen

Requirements: music and class participation

Number of players: 5 - 15 children

The leader will begin by playing background music, during which the students will be allowed to run freely, dance, play, etc. When the leader turns the volume down and says "frozen" everyone must stop and remain still, until the volume is turned back up again.

The game ends followed by a few questions. How did you feel during the game? What did you experience? Was it difficult to freeze when the volume was turned down? How do you feel about self-discipline? What did you learn?

After that, the children will be able to play a while more, and then withdraw from the space.

78.– The stopwatch

Requirements: a clock

Number of players: 5 – 15 children

The children will sit in a circle. The leader will make a list of various things to do, indicating a time for each one. Example: sweep 2 minutes, jump 1 minute, tidy up 4 minutes, read 2 minutes, sing 3 minutes, among others. The leader will be in charge of timing the students and when they say "change", the children will quickly change activities.

This is how the game will be carried out; the leader will indicate the action and each student will execute it.

At the end, a space for reflection will be opened. What did you think of the activity? Did you enjoy it? How did you feel? Was it difficult to finish on time? Was it difficult to adapt to the changes? What did you learn?

79.- The behavior table

Requirements: sheet of bond paper, pencils, markers, tape and expression faces.

Number of players: 5 - 15 children

The children will stand in a circle with their leader to attend the The children will stand in a circle and will be given a sheet of bond paper, pencils and markers. They must make a list of all their daily tasks, from the moment they wake up until they go to bed. In it, they must also include the tasks and responsibilities that their daily assignments require.

The children will begin to work on the assignment, putting together their list and adding color to it if they desire. Once finished, they will tape it on the wall. Then, one by one they will read their list out loud, placing an expression face next to the task that their exposing. If the task was completed then they will place a happy face, if it was half finished then they will place a serious face, and if they did not finish it at all then they will place a sad face.

The game comes to an end with a space for reflection. How did you feel? What did you think of the game? What can you improve? How could you improve? Why is it important to be self-disciplined? What did you learn from the game?

The teacher will conclude the class by emphasizing the importance of self-discipline in order to fulfill all responsibilities.

80.- Dictated drawings

Requirements: Paper, pencils and colors

Requirements: 5 - 15 children

The children will sit in a circle next to the leader and listen to the directions of the game.

The teacher will begin by reading out loud certain descriptions that the students must carefully listen to and draw. The teacher must be very detailed, for example: let's draw a dog, its silhouette, its pointy ears, its furry face, its big eyes, its curly tail, etc. The students must draw exactly what the leader is describing.

This is how each and every drawing will be carried out. At the end, the students will be able to share their creations with the rest of the class and a space for reflection will open.

How did you feel? What did you think of the descriptions? Did you like it? Had you done it before? Did it seem very complex? What do you think of your final creation? What was the learning acquired?

Time ends and they say goodbye until the next meeting.

.

Games to
improve adaptability

Life is constantly throwing curveballs at us, and we must be prepared to adjust to the changes that come with it. Adaptability skills allow us to quickly and efficiently respond to new circumstances and embrace challenges better.

81.– Hot potato

Requirements: a potato

Number of players: 5 - 15 children

The children will sit in a circle next to each other; their leader will sit with them to explain the activity and begin.

The game will consist in passing around a potato while the leader repeats "hot potato, hot potato, who has the hot potato, if you have the hot potato, you are out". When the leader finishes the phrase, the last person holding the potato is out and must stand in the middle of the circle.

The game will continue like this until there is only one person left in the circle, and that person will be the winner.

The activity will conclude with the following directed questions: What did you think of the game? How did you feel? How did it feel when you lost? What did you learn from the game?

After the activity, they can leave the space.

82.- The apartment

Requirements: class participation

Number of players: 5 - 15 children

The leader will divide the children into groups of three; two of them will hold hands above their heads and will be the apartment, the other team will be located inside them and will be the tenant.

The game will consist of the following: when the leader says "apartment", those who were the apartment will run away and quickly look for another tenant. When the leader says "tenants" all the tenants will leave their apartment in search of another.

This is how the game will be carried out, and as many times as the leader indicates. The activity concludes with a time for reflection. What did you think of the game? How did you feel? Did you adapt quickly to the requested changes? Why is it necessary to develop this ability? What lesson have you learned?

83.- Dancing with balloons

Requirements: balloons, string and music

Number of players: 5 15 children

The leader will first tie string around each balloon. Then, place the children in a circle and give them two balloons. They will tie the balloon string around each ankle and the guide will play music for them to dance throughout the space.

The game will consist of the children trying to explode their classmates' balloons with their feet while they dance; some will succeed and others will not. The children whose balloons explode will have to sit down. The game will continue until only one person remains with their balloons intact.

The activity will conclude with directed questions. What did you think of the activity? How did you feel? Was it hard to pop your classmates' balloons? What did you learn from the game?

Time is up, until the next opportunity to meet again.

84.- Changing Chairs

Requirements: chairs

Number of players: 5 - 15 children

The children will be divided into groups of three and will listen to the guidelines of the game. The teacher will locate three chairs with their respective numbers 1, 2, 3; these chairs will be destined for the children who manage to answer more questions.

The leader will begin with a list of questions, for which the children must give the correct answer. The child who answers the most questions will sit in chair 1; the child who follows will sit in chair 2, and the other in chair 3. However, if one of them were to make a mistake in their answers, they would go down a place, or if they got more correct answers, they would go up.

After a few questions, the next group will pass and so on, until everyone has finished participating. At the end, they will close with the following questions: How did you feel during the game? What did you think of the game dynamics? What did it feel like to change places? What did you learn?

Class ends and everyone leaves the space.

Games to promote active participation

Many children tend to be a bit shy and have a hard time actively participating in activities when they are in a group. It is important to develop an atmosphere where the child feels confident and secure, enabling them to take part in the different activities.

85.- The king asks

Requirements: class participation

Number of players: 5 - 15 children

The children will be placed in a large circle and will choose a child who will be the king; at his orders everyone must respond.

The king will stand in the center of the circle and the rest of the children will remain around. The king will begin making his requests for the other children to begin the search. Example: if the king asks that they bring him a shoe, everyone must run and look for a shoe, if the king asks them to run around the table then they must oblige, and so forth. This is how the game will take place.

After a while, the leader can change the king or name a queen until the game is over. The idea is for everyone to participate. Once finished, there will be a space for reflection.

What did you think of the game? Was it fun? How did you feel? How did it feel to be named king or queen? How did you feel obeying the king's orders? What was the learning acquired?

Even when children are given the opportunity to play, not all like the idea of actively participating. Motivating children to overcome their social anxiety will help them to better adapt in their environment.

?

86.– Class lecture

Requirements: class participation

Number of players: 5 – 25 children

The children will sit in a circle next to the guide listen to the leader give a lecture on a topic that is of interest to them. However, the guide will then select someone to take over and continue giving the class. That person will be given a few minutes to prepare and organize what they are going to say, and also make a list of questions and answers that they'll later ask the rest of the class.

Once prepared, the student will take the floor and carry out the lecture. When they have finished, the teacher will randomly select students to pass to the front of the room and answer the questions on the list.

The teacher can then choose another child and repeat the activity.

The activity ends with the following questions: What did you think of the game? How did you feel actively participating? What did you think of your classmates' responses? What did you learn?

87.– Sing along

Requirements: music

Number of players: 5 – 15 children

All the children will stand in a big circle and the guide will explain the game. It will consist of singing along to the lyrics of a song that the leader will play. When the volume is turned down they will have to continue singing alone; sometimes different children will be selected to stand in the center of the group and continue singing. Everyone must participate.

Afterwards, they will proceed to sit down and give room for reflection. What did you think of the game? How did you feel singing? Were you afraid to stand in the center and sing? Would you like to repeat the activity? What have you learned from this activity?

 Class is dismissed; the children can stay and continue listening to music.

88.- Complete the sentence

Requirements: group of children

Number of players: 5 - 15 children

The children will sit one next to the other and listen carefully to directions.

The activity will consist of the class creating a story by completing the missing parts of the sentences. The leader will start reading and each child will add what they think is missing. Example: the leader begins, "Mary went out to the field..." and someone will add, "...to play with Lola...", and another child will continue, "...but she didn't know it was going to rain".

Everyone will have a chance to participate until the story is complete. After, the leader will reread the story with all the added phrases.

The activity is finalized and a space for reflection is opened. What did you think of your participation? What do you think about how the story began and how it ended? How do you feel? Was the game productive? What did you learn?

Time is up and everyone can leave the place.

Games to develop leadership skills

Leadership skills allow children to have confidence in taking control and solving problems that arise. A good leader must be able to work in a team, help and guide others and think of creative solutions.

89.– Who is at the helm?

Requirements: class participation

Number of players: 5 - 15 children

The children will sit in a circle and pretend that they are on a boat. Then they will choose who will be at the helm, and that person will be in charge of giving each child a task to do on the boat. One person will have to carry the life jackets, another will be in charge of the anchor, someone else will take care of the passengers, etc.

The game begins and the children start their journey. Suddenly the teacher says "Who is at the helm?" and the ship begins to sink. The child at the helm must guide the team and give orders to prevent the ship from sinking. The captain will be in charge of deciding everyone's fate.

When the game is over there will be space for reflection. What did you think of the activity? How did you feel? What did you think of the captain's leadership skills? Could anything else have been done to save the ship? (This is in case the ship has sunk.) Were all the decisions the most appropriate? Did the captain need more help? What did you learn from the game?

Class ends and the children withdraw from the space.

.

90.–Recreation

Requirements: music

Number of players: 5 – 15 children

The children will stand in a circle. The game will consist of doing physical activity that, at first will be directed by the teacher, but then someone else will be in charge of taking over the leadership position.

The game starts when the music begins; the leader will stand in the center and guides all the movements that the children must do. When the music stops, the leader will choose a child to be in charge of leading the activity. There will be as many rounds as desired so that all the children can participate.

Once the game ends, there will be room for reflection. How did you feel during the game? How do you feel now? What did you think of the activity? Did you enjoy leading the activity? What did you learn?

91.- Look for the leader

Requirements: Scarves

Number of players: 5 - 15 children

The children will be divided into small groups of 5, and each will choose a leader for their group. They will be given a reasonable amount of time to share with each other and for the selected leader of the group to memorize the names of each member.

Once the time is up, the children in each group will cover their eyes with a scarf, while their leaders will locate themselves in strategic places. Then, each leader will begin to call the members of their team by their names; these in turn, will try to identify their leader's voice and walk towards them.

Once all the members have reunited as a group, they will uncover their eyes and sit in a circle to reflect.

What did you think of the game? How did you feel? Was it very difficult to locate your leader? Did you quickly identify their voice? What did you learn?

Conclude the activity with some free time for play before leaving the place.

Made in the USA
Las Vegas, NV
20 November 2024

12160256R00075